feeling

Tamera Birkett

BookLeaf
Publishing

love is only a feeling © 2023 Tamera Birkett

All rights reserved.

No part of this publication may be reproduced, stored in a retrieval system, or transmitted, in any form or by any means, electronic, mechanical, photocopying, recording, or otherwise, without the prior written permission of the presenters.

Tamera Birkett asserts the moral right to be identified as the author of this work.

Presentation by *BookLeaf Publishing*

Web: www.bookleafpub.com

E-mail: info@bookleafpub.com

ISBN: 9789357216456

First edition 2023

For the people who hate that they love love

ACKNOWLEDGEMENT

A plant does not simply need oxygen
it requires nourishment, food
exposure to the elements is what we forget to include
Stimulation of the sun
Fiery motivation
To push and encourage reformation
Water, too
Emotional support,
to hydrate these grande expectations

A simple seed in the dirt will only get you so far
Especially when you don't acknowledge the
signs that were with you from the start.

Fire and Water; The only two who can make my words stronger.

Tamera Birkett, 2022

PREFACE

Exploring the complex ideas of love in various forms of relationships. Familial, romantic, and self-love. "LOVE IS ONLY A FEELING" merely exists to track the process of emotions when not only faced with first love but first loss- a deteriorating perception. We are in the past, present, and future of the meaning of devotion and how it often changes without even truly noticing until we have arrived on the other side. Even when you want it to be more, love is only a feeling, especially when attached to other emotions that complicate this raw, underlying emotion.

My Letter back Home

Treasured,

The air is different across the pond.
Romantic- From a distance, I can see the navy clouds
Hugging the shy moon
It makes me wonder
if you can see it too.
I digest slowly By the window
I wonder if you're lonely,
I wonder when you'll phone me
I wish there was more time in the
Day - the world is constantly spinning
But when I focus on the moon and stars
I know you're somewhere. Grinning.
I hope you read my roundabout version of a "hi"
Just hoping you'll reply
Please, don't miss me too much while I'm away
I need this time to figure out who I am
It is my new dawn-
Who am I to you?
Who am I to myself?
I need to know before everything I once knew
Is gone.
It's goodbye for now.

Just don't let your heart stray too far
Don't let it roam.
It will be 365 cycles
until I am home...

Where Do You Go When You Die

It is the oldest question in the book
It requires an answer of depth and emotion
But
I will be able to tell with one look.
Is it this moment in time?
Or an everlasting challenge?

I sincerely wonder if the lighthouse
still shines,
If there's a safe home
-A quaint place to call my own...

So much distance between the wind and the water
It gives me hope that I won't
Go under-

So I ask again, out loud.
A question with no correct answer

What type of life is it
That you choose
to walk the world alone
with no one to call
your muse

Falling

Deeper and deeper
Into the earth's core
beneath the water
30,000 feet-
Beneath the seas floor
It's the discovery of a new
Way
It's been on my mind,
it's such a fine line
How vast our kind
is-
to see so clearly, When our receptors are blind

I am looking for a new world
That I search for each day
In everyone. Everywhere I go
It is
What keeps me going-
A whisper in my ear
So warm and low
When you said,
"That keeps me searching for a heart."
You meant
Though the process is slow
Dig Deeper

You have 20,000 more
Feet to go

Love 2 Fast

Oh, I can hear a symphony Of violins
When our eyes meet
The stories of the sun and moon
A tragedy, So sweet
What could it be…
Is it what it seems?
Maybe it's the night.
Maybe it's a dream…
Outside is dark...
Though your eyes are so bright
It gives me an undeniable spark.

Even on my worst day,
I wonder if you're mine
Even when I no longer love
You still begged me to stay
With one simple look

It made me question whose love this belonged to
Anyway…

Again, Again and Again,
Every time I try to force my love
Two shattered half hearts
Are left in pain

10-10-10

I took a drive
took an hour of my time
I wondered what it meant -To be me
Versus - What it should be
It's feeling less like a quest
Rather than...I'm obsessed
With a life that doesn't exist
Nothing really goes to plan
Many memories- Missed
My fantasy feels so real
When I close my eyes
It's more than an hour of my time
Ten thoughts
Ten dreams
Ten - "what does it mean?"
Is there more?
Is it too much that I am asking for?
I wished dearly we could go back to before
I just don't know what that is anymore

I took a drive
It took hours off my life.

Love Is Hate

Forgive me if I'm wrong-
It's been a while... I can't say how long-

It's true, it's true-
I've been avoiding you
I was waiting for the moment
I felt brand new

I can't help but notice how you look so tense
Allow me to offer
My one, two cents
I can't help but look away when I see you in pain
To feel beautiful
Has such a price to pay

Please!
Don't look at me that way
After All, it's the life I chose
To keep my mind at bay

Its gaze pulled me near, rolling her eyes
Disappointed- I almost shed a tear
Because it is to the image in my head,
Which I adhere

Love me, Love you, Love who you choose
I don't know when you became this way
What is your excuse...

I wish it was *that* easy
to pinpoint my flaws
and scream," VENI, VIDI, VICI."

when I go home,
I realize
I am still me.

It makes me sad
to be owned by your reflection
when all you wish to see in the mirror
is perfection

Ghost of the Lovers Past

The last time he was seen was just last week, though
It feels as if we had spoken many moons ago
His family misses him dearly; that is what they tell me all the time
I just can't believe I didn't notice sooner, but he is the definition of a ghost
A phantom, a soul unclaimed- I always wondered if he could feel pain
I realized that he lives in the back of my mind, a faded memory of the past

When I picked up the phone to dial, I remembered we hadn't spoken in 10 years past.
My brain and my hand fight with one another about dialing the phone, although
I can feel his brain is on fire, like mine, but I can't tell if it's all him- or just blanket pain.
It pains me; I keep pushing to mend a life that was so sweet not long ago
Contemplating whether things will ever get better or if they'll follow me as a ghost
Despite neither nor has claimed the blame- it's true how I spend most of my time

He reaches for the phone and pauses… will you look at the time
He wonders if I saw him on the street... Would I say hi or walk past?
He was saved by the bell, his mental decline. He walks the halls like a ghost.
When he closes his eyes, I know he can hear my voice so clearly, though
I know he despises such a sound- me crying only one year ago.
He looks out the window, wondering what I think... if I can even feel pain.

He couldn't even meet my eyes; he left me so suddenly and in pain
I can't help but feel deceived by such a crime, bombarding me with truths at this time
I felt betrayed; he mentioned his regret, how he wished we'd met months ago
It's only when I look at him do I wish he was left in a vault in the past
I looked at him kindly, so disappointed… though
My glare was cold, detached. I knew he was afraid; his skin was translucent- 1 of a ghost.

He saw her as a shell of what she used to be, a poltergeist, a bitter ghost.
He held his heart and took a few steps back; only he could feel her pain.

He stared empathetically, happy to see me although
He was scared to meet her - he closed his eyes and went back in time
He had regret in his eyes for stopping her in her tracks; if only he had just walked past
He knew how upset I was; he should have been here sooner, a long time ago

I wish I could forgive and forget, but this pain was formed years ago
But perhaps I walk through memories, from a shadowland, like a ghost
Have I let days, months, and years heal the pain at last? Am I who I was in the past?
Of some sort, I can feel my heart start to thaw. Could it be... Departing pains?
I wonder what it means when I think about all the good times
My stare softened time after time for some reason, though

I throw my hands up in defeat; though I've been hurt, I've forgiven directions from some time ago.
I rather live in the present and focus on a new time- instead of living in purgatory as a ghost.

I know many languages of love that could cause me pain, but they are languages amassed- dead and long in the past.

Trip 2 the Moon

Closed eyes
Long days feel like short nights
My head feels light,
When you're in my presence
I breathe you in
I cough and cry
I can't finish my -

Sentences are short with you
So I lay my head back.
There are stars in my vision
And tonight, the moon is blue.

Only I can lose time
And space
When it's just us two

Under the rocks and rubble
Something new starts to flood
A calm wave washes over me
A new piece, buds

Forgive me
For the old memory
Of my anxiety

Time and space
Out of this world
With you
As we defy gravity

On this trip to the moon
I fear not, mortality
Because back in reality
 open my eyes
I know you will leave me soon.

C'est Toujours Toi (With Translation)

mon coeur est remplie
c'est vous que j'adore
plus que ma propre vie
in a world of darkness
you make it easy to see
tu illumines mon âme
you illuminate my life
in a way that cuts more profound than a knife
quand nos cœurs se touchent, ma peau se met à danser
Je me perds dans tout ce que tu es
Je me demande si c'est ma seule chance
à l'amour,
à la vie,
que dirais-tu?
accepteriez-vous?

Translation:

My heart is full
It is you that I adore
More than my own life
In a world of darkness
You make it easy to see
You illuminate my soul
You illuminate my life
In a way that cuts more profound than a knife
I lose myself in everything that you are
I wonder if this is my only chance
at love,
at life,
what would you say?
would you agree?

Seasons Of Love

The most serene sea,
a wave so quiet and so sweet
time is bittersweet

A walk in the park
the simple crunch of the leaves,
 is more than it seems

I close my eyes and
inhale the crisp autumn air
there is hope somewhere.

And just like I thought,
Cold has taken over now
Ice, to freeze my heart

When will this love thaw
Me, I wish to feel something,
To be left in awe

Bloom! I see the sun
A moment from my dream
Oh, to feel the heat

I love how the seasons
Are consistent.
They are all the same.
Rather the personas who live through them
Never seem to remain-

love is a venomous snake

I was scared to open my eyes
When they are closed
Everything is still
And silence is the prize
It's challenging to come by
But not one thing could stop
My barricaded heart
It raised me
It heard me
And one day, it betrayed me
Like a venomous snake in the garden
Confined amidst a blissful bout of silence
I almost didn't stand a chance
One bite
Is all it takes
For the toxin to sink into my blood
Plaguing my brain with questions from my heart
Like a flash flood

In the blink of an eye,
The noise is back
Asking me, how long is forever?
For me
It is forever and ever- an infinity of time
in which we are linked together
To love is like having

Open heart surgery
Being unable to detect an invisible tether

Venom does mysterious things to a heart covered in cobwebs
The ability to lose control over the strongest muscle
When your head tells you to stop though
Your heart is in an internal shuffle
And even after all is said and done
Just when you think
There is nothing left at stake
You feel another pang of guilt
As teeth sink into you
Just know love is a venomous snake

Living In Colour

I sat before power today
Scared and afraid
Of the certain
Way they talk
I stay hidden behind a mask
so you couldn't hear a squawk

I fell in love with a world
Who can't love me
The same way-
It wasn't until I removed my glasses
Did I realize how gray
The world was
For someone who just wants to be free-

Who looked like me…
It's quite hard to please.
When the ones you trusted
Cut you by your knees.

I chose, not
to walk alone
But it seems that certain ones
Refuse to understand
This was no choice of my own

I close my eyes
Hark! the rhythmic march
Under the guise
Of an oasis of freedom
The clock stood still and
my -
ocardium dies

I, too, had a dream
But I woke up too soon
That seems to be the theme...
How could something so
Beautiful
Be so hard to achieve?
Living in colour-
Where you fight for what
You believe
Where nothing comes easy
Though you wish your dreams
Were placed at your feet

If there's a chance
It's more than a fantasy
More than a dream
I tip my hat to the king
Because nothing is as it seems

Tell Me, Love

LOVE,
Tell me,
How should I feel-
Is it a hopeless endeavor
Or is cupid sneaky yet clever
LOVE,
Tell me!
It happens to whoever

It is not the truth; I fear
love
But the repercussions of
Submerging in my own heartbreak
Will I be colder,
LOVE,
Tell me how I can be so happy
When I am only adored in the
Eyes of my beholder

LOVE,
Tell me how to know
Teach me
To be brave
Open my soul
So I cannot hope in hell

And take this virgin heart to
The grave

Tell me what I want to hear
Love,
Tell me

Love is real
Everywhere
All the time
Tell me, Love

Letter To Her

I will never hear my name again
if it doesn't come from your voice
I'll never say your name in vain

It's quite an easy choice.

A name of beauty
this poem is for thee

In a world full of darkness
It is only you

Who can set me free.

Island of Pain

You live on an island of pain
a short distance, detached
but you'll never be the same

Consumed by your trauma
that you never adequately healed
you have no choice but to
Prolong new drama

I want you there, but you make it so hard
You can't be here for us
while also leaving me scarred

The narrative is exhausting
and I need my own life
my resources
used up, gone
you don't know what you're costing
You scare me
You lie
I can't begin to understand why

Please!
I beg
Please don't cry

it pains my heart
tightens my chest
to leave, but I wish you the best

Love Is Only A Feeling

Cursed by the love I dream about
I have decided to throw the towel in
No ifs, No buts- No whys
My mind is clear of any doubt

How could I have lived so recklessly
With someone else's heart
Yes, I'm changing
for the good
-It is not romantic
But I know it is smart

I am doing this for no one but myself
He stopped by once with flowers,
left them at the door
I waited until he was gone
And I stared at them for hours

I am weak,
Can't you see
But I put a bandaid on my heart
And it started healing
This is how I know it is not a natural feeling
"an intense feeling of deep affection"
I can't be tricked

It is merely psychosis
A common infection

Yes, I am familiar with such passion
Just hold me before you go
That is all of me that I can ration
That is all our love has to show.

Reverence

he lives in her
he lives in his own world
which is unheard

he lives in my head
he lives in my dreams
together we live off the beaten path
in a land full of trees

he lives in the sound the birds make
he lives in the rush of the river
his voice is alive in my thoughts - a voice that
makes me shiver

he lives in my eyes
captivating me
with lies
they hold me tight
until I can't breath
he lives only for me
I am all he can see

I love to muse about
if he's real or not
I see him when I close my eyes

I whisper his name
across the sea of lights
I wonder if he sits at night

yearning,   yearning,   yearning

I whisper his name
and I whisper again

I can tell he feels the same
by the way he calls the world ours
But it can't fix my scars.

Then There Was 1

I awoke before my body
and was trapped by the
truth
the great reveal
how much I care
and never speak
how much I feel
but have never healed

Do you know me?
Can you show me?
I can't seem to remember
I am old, not young
a birthday in the fall?
I am bold
But still feel small.

show me
I know you know me
did you notice how much time has passed
since you'd seen me stand on my own two feet?
Did I miss it?
Did you call defeat?

I awoke before my body
and I got lost
I searched for you with my eyes closed
but our paths never crossed.

I sit before the shell of a life once lived,
watching what has been outgrown
I hold back a groan and stand on my two feet

I have to finish this journey on my own...

o.p.a

a rusty streetlight
just steps away
turns on when I walk by
I can't help but wonder why

is it absurd
that I stand under the light
hoping to feel its warmth
on the coldest nights
with salt crunching under my boot
I can't help but hope
It's you.

I can hear your voice
though we haven't met
you ask me how I'm doing
and I respond that,
"I'm a wreck."

It's only when that light flickers on
I know you're near
from way up above
with the powers that be

I can feel your warmth as you watch over me

Infatuation

You've been doing well
I can see you now,
Standing before me
Words flood my mouth
Before my brain can allow
to process just what I feel
What I see
What I so dearly want to be

Don't you see…
It's interesting what happens
when you allow life to play through.
You just need to focus on you
And the dreams you plan to pursue

It doesn't matter if you haven't gotten a clue
What matters is the process
And what you know is true
Yes, you've been doing well, More than you're able to tell
But I can see it so clearly
How you stand tall, your chin high
No a single doubt in your eye
You make me proud
When you turn around to the crowd

There is not one single eye
That is left dry

I am in awe
Struck by love,
I wonder what it all means
It happened overnight,
But it is so strong,
I cannot put up a fight

I asked for a noble core.
And the universe delivered.
You don't even see me.
But strangely,
It intrigues me more

You asked if I was whole; I'm not
You asked if I love, but I haven't been taught
Does that change anything?
I asked if I was yours.
Though I am not even mine
I asked if you could give me more, and you did
But what do you do with love
When you have it
You don't want it anymore

There's nowhere left to turn.
My mistake was grave.
I can't take it back.

It wasn't you
But the idea in my head
I so desperately crave

Is there a healing timeline?
When will we no longer be a shell of the vicious past
Will I ever look the same to you?
I am too scared to ask.
Lie to me,
The same way I once did to you
Let me know if those feelings are true

The Sun Will Rise Again

Do you ever wonder what could have been?
If I spoke from the heart
Maybe trusted my thoughts from within

Would I still live in regret?
Days pass
And it's me you start to forget.

I am restless when you're not here
I feel everything so deeply
That I get dizzy when you're near

Look me in the eyes
Tell me who you see
A lover, a woman, a friend
Tell me!
Then set me free…

They bent down
To my eye level
And simply said
"The Sun Will Rise Again"

Oh, tell me what it all means.
I can't let the sun die without saying what I please
I want nothing more than your love
They say nothing but with one look, I know they agree.

The sun has cast a dark shadow on my face
I know I am blind
Just because we do not belong to one another
Does not mean
Our hearts don't intertwine

Love is meant to be walked.
Like a fine line
It takes many heartbreaks to figure out
That time is divine

 sun - will rise again
And I believe it to be true
When we meet again
Yes, they will love me
But I'll love myself too.

CPSIA information can be obtained
at www.ICGtesting.com
Printed in the USA
BVHW051131130723
667186BV00016B/1513

9 789357 216456